Presented to

Mrs. Silua

On the occasion of

Cricket's Kindergarten Graduation

From

Cricket Henderson

Date

6-14-01

Published by Barbour Publishing, Inc.
P.O. Box 719
Uhrichsville, Ohio 44683
http://www.barbourbooks.com

 Member of the
Evangelical Christian
Publishers Association

Printed in China.

A Teacher's Heart

Colleen L. Reece and
Anita Corrine Donihue

BARBOUR
PUBLISHING, INC.

A Teacher's Heart

ADMONITION

Train a child in the way he should go,
and when he is old he will not turn from it.
PROVERBS 22:6, NIV

A Teacher's Heart

ACHIEVEMENT

Successful teachers are those who have lived well,
laughed often, and loved much;
who have gained the respect of intelligent persons
and the love of children;
who have filled their niches and accomplished their tasks;
who leave the world better than they found it—
whether by an improved poppy,
a perfect poem, or a rescued soul;
who never lacked appreciation of earth's beauty
or failed to express it;
who looked for the best in others
and gave the best they had.

Adapted from ROBERT LOUIS STEVENSON

A Teacher's Heart

A teacher's heart has many rooms.
Each needs a different key.
Love and caring unbolt some compartments.
Faith and prayer find a way into others.
Patience and compassion pick the locks
of tightly shuttered windows,
letting in the light of hope and encouragement.
Only then can lives be changed; teachers' and students',
Forever.

A teacher's heart has many rooms.
Each needs a different key,
designed by the Master Teacher
Who made the shores of the Sea of Galilee
His classroom and changed the world,
Forever.

INNER VISION

If you could see beneath the rumpled hair,
The pizza-stained shirt, behind the freckles.
If you could look inside a squirming body;
Dreamy eyes staring out the window,
What would you find?
A second Einstein? Another Michelangelo?
Or a child like every other child,
Longing for you to turn the key;
To set him free to become what he longs to be.

I LOVE YOU SPECIAL

The first time I met seven-year-old Lacey, she stole my heart. Her long, blond ponytail bounced behind her, reflecting her bubbly personality. Her blue eyes sparkled from behind thick, heavy glasses. And I soon learned that her sparsely toothed grin is a smile that doesn't quit.

Lacey has Down's Syndrome. In spite of her difficulty in learning quickly, she is curious and eager to try. She ran so fast during recess I could barely keep up. Everyone marveled at the way she performed flips and turns on the monkey bars. Friends from all classes flocked to her. Sometimes Lacey was overwhelmed and covered her eyes until I helped her escape from so much excitement. Before she did, she always hugged the other students, whom she genuinely loved.

Unlike the other kids, Lacey never called me Mrs. Donihue or Mrs. D.; she's always called me "Teach." At times she could be stubborn. Arms and legs crossed on the rug, she would refuse to do her work, but her pout would soon leave and her irresistible smile returned.

After three years with us, Lacey moved on to another school. I could barely contain the tears when we said good-bye. We had developed a special kind of love.

Lacey still has a corner of my heart. I keep her picture up and pray for her. Occasionally, she returns to visit our class. And one of my biggest thrills is when I'm in a store or restaurant and hear her unmistakable strong, husky voice call, "Hey, Teach!"

The world around us seems to stop. Lacey dashes toward me and I brace myself. Arms and legs fly around my waist and neck in a vise-like hug that I joyfully return. Then I hear the words that warm and melt my heart. "I love you, Teach. I love you special."

I am here for a purpose.
I came from heaven above
With something great to give you:
A special kind of love.

A Teacher's Heart

If you can bring
one moment of
happiness into the life of a child,
you are a coworker
with God.

FOLLOWING STARS

Ralph Waldo Emerson said, "Hitch your wagon to a star." The Three
Wise Men probably had no wagon, but they followed the Star of the
East. It led them to the world's greatest treasure, Jesus, lying in a
manger near Bethlehem. Surely God smiles when dedicated teachers
encourage their students to follow their own particular stars.

DID THEY KNOW?

Did the disciples know as they sat at Jesus' feet and learned life's
most important lessons, that one day they would pick up the torch of
his teachings and carry light into a dark world?

What teachers instill in young minds is the spark from which gen-
erations of flaming torches of truth may be lit.

HEART AND SPIRIT

At six weeks of age, she became ill. Doctors seriously and tragically erred in her treatment. As a result, she lost her eyesight and could only distinguish darkness from light.

In spite of her disability, her parents and teachers encouraged her to try as many things as possible during childhood. She loved to climb trees and ride horses bareback. Remarkably, she memorized huge portions of the Bible. Later, she studied at the Northwest Institute for the Blind, then remained at the school to teach history and language.

She weighed no more than a hundred pounds as a young lady. Not attractive by conventional standards, her wit, grace, and charm captured listeners when she spoke. Her compassion for the needy, for street people, and for children made her lovely in heart and spirit.

Her music and poetry filled our world. She wrote between 8000 and 9000 hymns and at seventy-one, penned one of her best-loved hymns, "Saved by Grace." Her name was Fanny Crosby.

Father, help us all to see
beyond our limitations.

PEBBLE ON THE SHORE

I do not know what I may appear to the world;
but to myself I seem to have been only
like a boy playing on the seashore,
and diverting myself in now and then
finding a smoother pebble or a pretty shell,
whilst the great ocean of truth lay
all undiscovered before me.

SIR ISAAC NEWTON

A Teacher's Heart

ONCE A TEACHER,
ALWAYS A TEACHER

Mom found her many years of teaching elementary school invaluable even after she retired. She saw examples for life in even the smallest incidents.

One day our large orange and white cat clawed at the screen door and meowed.

Mom went to see what he wanted. There stood Felix (who in no way resembled the cartoon cat) proudly displaying his hunting prowess.

Mom gingerly disposed of the dead mouse, patted Felix, and exclaimed, "What a good cat you are!" He trotted at her heels, wearing a satisfied cat-smirk on his babyish face.

The next day Felix summoned her to view a dead mole, the results of his hunting in the vacant lot next to our house. Mom was impressed and said so.

The third day Felix went through the same rigmarole. Mom was beginning to tire of his rodent offerings. Which would it be today? Mouse or mole? She took one look and shook with laughter. Mighty hunter Felix had brought her a long and wiggling night crawler!

Mom didn't have the heart to erase the self-satisfied smile from his smug face. The cat got his petting and praise.

When she told me about it that night, she held her sides from laughing. "Isn't that just like some people?" she gasped when she could get her breath. "As proud of a tiny achievement as a large one."

I thought of times I had visited Mom's classroom. I'd seen shocky-headed urchins walk away from their teacher's desk, heads high, eyes shining. "Yes," I agreed. "But remember, you always praised your students' efforts equally, the same way you praised Felix for his mouse, mole, and night crawler. The child who showed the slightest improvement received the same warm approval as those making A's. And that's why they all loved you."

Mom just smiled.

The orange and white cat in her lap shot me a triumphant glance and purred louder than ever.

A Teacher's Heart

Be prepared in season and out of season. . .
2 TIMOTHY 4:2, NIV

WORDS

If there be words of kindness
words of praise
words of encouragement
Speak them now.
Listen to your heart and respond.
Someone, somewhere, is waiting for your words.

LOST OPPORTUNITIES

A teacher once thought she would write and congratulate a co-worker on a special achievement. Instead, she grew busy and failed to do so. She excused herself by saying her letter would never be missed in the wealth of congratulations the other teacher would be sure to receive.

Some time later, she met her fellow instructor and apologized. To her amazement and dismay, the hardworking teacher had not received even one congratulatory note of commendation or appreciation.

John Ruskin once said two sad things happen when we fail to praise. We run the risk of driving a person from the right road for want of encouragement, and we deprive ourselves of the happy privilege of rewarding deserving labor.

Lord, may we always be quick to praise,
slow to criticize.

Genius is
undiscovered gold.
Talented is
the teacher who
struggles, finds, and
helps students develop it.

The man without purpose is
like a ship without a rudder—a waif,
a nothing, a no-man.
Have a purpose in life, and having it,
throw such strength of mind and muscle
into your work as God has given you.

THOMAS CARLYLE

Biographical note: Thomas Carlyle certainly knew adversity. He experienced one of the worst things that can happen to an author. After completing the first volume of his book, *The French Revolution,* his friend John Stuart Mill borrowed the manuscript. By accident, Mill's housemaid burned the manuscript! Carlyle didn't give up, however. He rewrote the book, largely from memory. It was finally published in 1837.

The next time the computer eats your lesson plans, remember Thomas Carlyle!

LEARNING TO MULTIPLY

The first Sunday my husband and I visited our new church, we were made to feel welcome, but something was missing. The tiny congregation, made up mostly of older people, had no children. We knew God had led us to this church. It was plain to see we were needed. Everyone longed to hear the sound of children's laughter echo through the building.

What could I do to help? I already taught school during the week and worked nights at a second job. Still, I felt God's tugging. Could He be leading me to teach the children we hoped would come? Where would I find the physical strength? Most of all, where would the kids come from?

A young mother and her two-year-old daughter Sierra began attending church. Dark, tightly curled ringlets framed the little girl's warm brown eyes and irresistible smile. I fell hopelessly in love with Sierra. Each time I turned around, she had her arms outstretched, waiting for me to pick her up.

God, there is only this one child, I prayed. *Can we reach more? Please help us multiply into many children.*

The following spring a vision for a Vacation Bible School struck me. And I knew I was the only one who could direct it. And though it was summer vacation, with my second job I would still have to function on four to five hours of sleep each night if I directed the week-long VBS. I prayed for strength and we launched into the program. Some said we couldn't do it, but our church's grandmas and grandpas showed up in force to go door knocking, then mustered their energy, skills, and do what was needed. Kids came. We were successful. At the end of the week, we had a church school promotional picnic.

Next came the question: who would teach the Primary/Junior class? We didn't even have teaching materials. Feeling nudged, I committed to six months. I dug remnants of teaching materials out of storage and poured my heart into the program. Before long we averaged fifteen to twenty kids each week.

Less than a year later, I watched six eager Juniors and one older brother tell of their love for God and be baptized. I was so happy I cried and thanked God.

Now the once-quiet halls of our church ring with children's laughter after worship. And when I feel that familiar tug at my skirt, I gather little Sierra into my arms. I can hardly wait for the day she is old enough to join my class, for I will continue teaching. With God's help, not only the children, but my commitment to love and teach has multiplied.

A Teacher's Heart

DUTY BOUND AND HONOR BOUND

I am not bound to win,
but I am bound to be true.
I am not bound to succeed,
but I am bound to live by the light that I have.
I must stand with anybody that stands right,
stand with him while he is right,
and part [company] with him when he goes wrong.

ABRAHAM LINCOLN

MESSAGE FROM A PRESIDENT

The Bible is the book of all others to be read at all ages and in all conditions of human life. . .I speak as a man of the world to men of the world, and I say to you, "Search the Scriptures."

JOHN QUINCY ADAMS

OPPORTUNITY

They do me wrong,
who say I come no more,
When once I knock
and fail to find you in;
For every day I stand
outside your door,
And bid you wake,
and rise to fight and win.

WALTER MALONE

A Teacher's Heart

FROM SEED TO HARVEST

Ben entered the huge multipurpose room of the church where the Christian Education conference was to be held. Electrical zeal and enthusiasm filled the air and Ben sensed the unmistakable presence of the Lord. But even after thirty years, he loyally clung to the small-town church where he taught church school.

A handsome middle-aged man eagerly approached Ben and smothered him in a bear hug. His humble, tender gaze searched the elderly teacher's face. His voice cracked and tears glistened in his eyes. "How are you, Ben? I am so happy to see you," he said.

Ben gripped Randy's hands. Looking at the face of the caring, dynamic pastor, Ben could still see that of a troubled teen. He remembered how thirty years earlier, Randy had almost lost sight of his calling to the ministry, how a friend's new red convertible and successful job had tempted the student facing mid-college burnout. Randy knew that if he left college, he would have plenty of money and he could trade in that old Volkswagon for a better car.

But God led Ben to spend hours with the troubled young man. After intense prayer, Randy exchanged material desires and regained his vision for God's ministry. He continued his studies and became what God wanted him to be: a caring, dynamic pastor, whose congregation numbered more than 5000.

INFLUENCE

He who is firm in will,
moulds the world to himself.

JOHANN WOLFGANG VON GOETHE

FLY BALL

Eight-year-old Anthony watched the kids play kickball. Anthony cheered and clapped his hands. Each time there was a catch, kick, or home run, he strained at his wheelchair seat belt, clapping and kicking with excitement. How he longed to be in that game!

Then it happened. The ball landed smack in Anthony's lap. He grabbed it with both hands. His brown eyes glowed and a bright smile lit up his face. Although he couldn't speak, Anthony showed what he could do. With a mighty heave, he sailed the ball across the diamond to home base!

The other kids were shocked, then excited. They all cheered wildly. Everyone knew Anthony loved ball games. He went to pro baseball games with his family and watched every game he could on TV. But what the kids didn't know was that Anthony and his dad spent many hours together playing catch in the park and in the family's backyard.

Soon Anthony was made pitcher. He not only pitched well, he put several people out. When his turn came to kick, one of the other kids helped him. Then Anthony flew from base to base in his wheelchair while his team cheered him on.

Even though the game went a little slower, everyone—especially Anthony—had more fun and all showed good team spirit. If you ask, you'll find that Anthony and his team are always ready for another game.

There never shall be
one lost good.
All we have willed or hoped
or dreamed of good
shall exist.

Robert Browning

SLOWING DOWN

The end of the world
does not depend on whether
we cleaned house or
washed dirty windows today.
(We just think it does!)

Work first, then rest.

JOHN RUSKIN

Foolish persons take better care
of their cars than of themselves.
Wise persons know they may have
many cars in their lifetimes,
but only one body.

A Teacher's Heart

SEVEN SIMPLE WAYS
TO REDUCE STRESS

1. A quiet, private devotion during recess.
2. A brisk walk before or after school, or at noon.
3. A warm cup of tea, anytime.
4. A quick stretch.
5. A change of classroom routine.
6. Driving to or from work a different way.
7. Imagining you are in Hawaii!

A Teacher's Heart

HANDLE WITH CARE

Ten-year-old Brian strolled into church school and slipped into his seat. Kris launched into her lesson with fervor and enthusiasm. The kids all responded well, yet each time she glanced at Brian, he appeared deep in thought.

Months passed. Each week the questions flew, especially from Brian. Kris took each question seriously, wondering what was going on in this special boy's head. One morning Kris asked if any of the kids knew what he or she wanted to do in the future. Some gave guesses or dreams, but no doubt clouded Brian's eyes.

"I'm going to be a preacher," he announced matter-of-factly. His clear, steady gaze met his teacher's, showing wisdom beyond his years. "That's why I want to learn so much. I know it's what I'm supposed to do."

Kris turned to Bible study and prayer to discover how she could best help Brian. The answers she received were simple: Handle with care. Don't expect more or less from him than anyone else. Don't use him as an example. Just teach him all he wants to learn, then show him how he can develop a close, growing, and personal relationship with his Lord. Hold him up in daily prayer. Be there when he needs to talk. Then step back and let the Lord work directly in Brian's life.

Jesus. . .said to them,
"Let the little children come to me,
and do not hinder them,
for the kingdom of God
belongs to such as these."

MARK 10:14, NIV

A Teacher's Heart

SOMEONE WHO CARED

I remember my principal, Mrs. Broderson, more than any educator in my early childhood years. I was only six and extremely shy when I first came to elementary school in Alderton, Washington. Before long, I discovered a warm and caring atmosphere throughout the school. My first-grade teacher was nice, but our principal Mrs. Broderson surpassed all. She frequented each classroom, generating positive but firm attitudes as she went. She appeared six feet tall to me, with muscles to handle the toughest boy or girl. Yet those same arms often hugged my tiny shoulders and showed me how much she cared.

Our principal insisted on manners, equality, and friendship among all the children, no matter our background or race. Patriotism ranked high and we learned the songs of our country well. Mrs. Broderson made recess fun, with a teacher always ready to rescue us, as needed.

At lunchtime, we gathered in small groups around long tables. A teacher stood at one end. We were asked to wait until everyone at our table was served before we ate. Then the teacher motioned for silence while she prayed the blessing on us and our food. We said, "Please," and "Thank you," and we asked "May I be excused?" before we left the table.

Mrs. Broderson's lessons followed me into adulthood. She armed me with three vital ingredients for life: love for God, self-control, and a good self-esteem. In turn, I carried these lessons over into day care centers I taught and directed. Now I am in a public school, but the teacher I work with and I pray silently before meals. We still plant seeds of love, kindness, and self-esteem. We still care and pray for each student.

Thank you, Mrs. Broderson, for all you did for me.

Goodness is the only investment
that never fails.

HENRY DAVID THOREAU

A Teacher's Heart

A HEART-FELT PRAYER
FOR TEACHERS

Lord, please bless all teachers.
Those who serve in public schools,
in private schools, through homeschooling.
And those who teach Your Word
in weekly church school classes.

All have chosen the paths
for which they feel they are best suited.
All have chosen the paths they feel
will best serve those they endeavor to teach.

Guide their feet that they may not stumble or lose the way,
lest those following after lose sight of the goal
and settle for a little knowledge when much is needed.

Help them instill in young hearts and minds
seeds of greatness, seeds of honor,
seeds of compassion, seeds of tolerance
seeds of courage to stand for what is right and denounce the wrong,
no matter how high the cost may be for speaking out.

Lord, please bless all teachers.
You have given them
the responsibility of training those who must grasp thefuture.
May it not be with uncertain hands, but with confidence.
May those You have called to point the way
first learn it from Thee.

Do your best to present yourself to God as one approved,
a workman who does not need to be ashamed and
who correctly handles the word of truth.
2 TIMOTHY 2:15, NIV

A Teacher's Heart

Sometimes when I am lonely, or discouraged, or sad, I withdraw from even my closest friends. I turn to others who have also touched my life: my book friends. They demand nothing from me but a little time. They welcome me into their worlds and include me in mental vacations my body is too busy to take. The Maine coast in summer. The Sea of Galilee, where Jesus walked. Magnificent mountains in Alaska. The magic of childhood revisited. A way of life now gone.

Knowing my book friends will always be there when I need them is a precious part of my life. I close a treasured book, return from my visit refreshed, and eagerly, joyously, look forward to meeting my book friends again.

Read the best books first, or
you may not have a chance to read them at all.

HENRY DAVID THOREAU

I would rather be a poor man in a garret with plenty of books
than a king who did not love reading.

THOMAS BABINGTON MACAULAY

WHO AM I?

Who am I, Lord, to teach children?
There is so much I do not know.
How can I teach the importance of loving?
I struggle so.

Lord, may my students always see
The real teaching come from Thee.

Love conquers all things;
let us too surrender to love.

VIRGIL

TWO BUILDERS

A builder builded a temple;
He wrought with care and skill;
Pillars and groins and arches
Were fashioned to meet his will;

And men said when they saw its beauty
"It shall never know decay.
Great is thy skill, oh builder,
Thy fame shall endure for aye."

A teacher builded a temple;
She wrought with skill and care;
Forming each pillar with patience,
Laying each stone with prayer.

None saw the unceasing effort;
None knew of the marvelous plan;
For the temple the teacher builded
Was unseen by the eyes of man.

Gone is the builder's temple;
Crumbled into the dust,
Pillar and groin and arches
Food for consuming rust;

But the temple the teacher builded
Shall endure while the ages roll;
For that beautiful, unseen temple
Was a Child's immortal soul.

AUTHOR UNKNOWN

A Teacher's Heart

TEACH ME,
MY GOD AND KING

Teach me, my God and King, In all things thee to see;
Teach me to be in everything; All thou wouldst have me be.

In all I think or say, Lord, may I not offend.
In all I do, be thou the way; In all be thou the end.

Each task I undertake, Though weak and mean to me,
If undertaken for thy sake; Draws strength and worth from thee.

Teach me, then, Lord, to bring, To all that I may be,
To all I do, my God and King, a consciousness of thee.

GEORGE HERBERT